Original title:
A Sanctuary of Soil

Copyright © 2025 Creative Arts Management OÜ
All rights reserved.

Author: Elliot Harrison
ISBN HARDBACK: 978-1-80581-852-6
ISBN PAPERBACK: 978-1-80581-379-8
ISBN EBOOK: 978-1-80581-852-6

## Roots Beneath the Surface

In the dirt, where gophers roam,
Worms host dance parties, feeling home.
Potatoes hide, they think they're sly,
While carrots chuckle, 'Oh my, oh my!'

The bugs are busy, raising their stakes,
Planning a fiesta for all their mates.
The soil's a stage, where secrets sway,
And plants gossip about the day!

## Whispering Earth

Underneath, the whispers hum,
The radishes giggle, 'Here we come!'
They hear the root beer talk, so sweet,
As turnips jiggle to the funky beat.

The pebbles cheer, they're always round,
Offering wisdom from the ground.
'What's the dirt on today's weather?'
They laugh and caress the seeds together.

## Embrace of the Ground

In the embrace where mosses lie,
The mushrooms caper, reaching high.
Mud pies baked by playful springs,
Frogs leap in with silly flings.

The grass tickles the ants on play,
Saying, 'Hey, what's the buzz today?'
Twirling dandelions dance and sway,
Sharing gossip in their own way!

**Tapestry of Terra**

In the tapestry where colors bloom,
Rabbits rave in a fluffy room.
The daisies gossip, 'Have you seen?
That sunflower? It's such a queen!'

Bees paint tunes on the fragrant air,
While the clovers laugh without a care.
The soil's a canvas, vibrant and wide,
Where nature's quirks take silly pride!

## The Quiet Below

In the earth where gophers play,
Worms are dancing every day.
Turtles wear their hats so bright,
Mole's got jokes, oh what a sight!

Rabbits hopping, trying to hide,
In the busy world, they collide.
Ants in suits march in a row,
Underneath the quiet show.

## Essence of the Underdirt

Grubs are munching on a treat,
It's just a leaf, but oh, so sweet!
Fungi giggle in a patch,
Mushrooms waving, what a catch!

Down below, it's quite the hive,
Mice in parties, oh, they thrive.
But no loud music, just the bass,
A soft vibe in this dark place.

## Veins of Vitality

Roots are tickling, what a scene,
Plants are gossiping, feeling keen.
Raccoons with their paws so sly,
Digging up secrets, oh my, oh my!

With a scoop and shuffle, they find,
The freshest snacks, so well-designed.
Under the dirt, the food parade,
Life's a feast that's never delayed!

## The Soil's Silent Song

Beneath the grass where shadows creep,
Napping critters, sound asleep.
In the thicket, laughter rings,
Who knew that dirt could share such things?

With a roll and tumble, bugs unite,
Waltzing 'neath that moonlit light.
And in this world, we often find,
The funniest tales that bind us kind.

## Tilling the Dreams

In the garden of giggles, I plant my seeds,
Where the rabbits wear glasses and share their creeds.
The carrots are dancing, the beets play the lute,
While the radishes gossip, dressed up in a suit.

Under the sun's laughter, the daisies bloom wide,
With stories of worms who take pride in their ride.
The cabbage is clever, with jokes up its leaves,
And the pumpkins compose songs, as autumnal thieves.

The tomatoes are blushing, where do they get that?
The cucumbers chuckle, they know they're quite pat.
In this quirky patch, where the funny things grow,
Every veggie's a character, putting on a show.

So let's raise a trowel, let's dig with a cheer,
In this playful plot, there's no room for a fear.
With the mud on our knees and the sun on our backs,
We'll harvest our laughter and share hearty snacks.

**Essence of the Elements**

In the soil, where the giggles and chuckles all meet,
The flowers wear sneakers, tapping their feet.
The rainclouds are playful, tossing drops with flair,
While the breezes blow kisses, flowing through the air.

The worms serenade, with a twist and a wiggle,
As butterflies join in, doing the jiggle.
The roots tell tall tales of adventures unheard,
While the bees buzz in chorus, uniting the herd.

The sunlight shines proudly, showcasing its rays,
Like a comedian on stage, it brightens our days.
With the rainbows as arches, we laugh and we play,
In this wild garden, where oddities sway.

So come and dig deep, with a smile on your face,
In this whimsical realm, there's plenty of space.
We'll plant all our dreams, watch them sprout joyfully,
In this creative chaos, we set our minds free.

## Soil's Silent Symphony

In the garden where worms do dance,
A little beetle takes his chance.
He plays a tune, a thump, a clank,
While the earthworms cheer from their hidden bank.

The daisies giggle, the carrots grin,
As root and riddle starts to spin.
With every squish and delightful squack,
The soil sings back, 'Hey! Watch your back!'

## Tranquil Terrains

In muddy shoes, we stomp around,
With squelchy sounds, we play profound.
The grass a-swirling, the daisies too,
Are laughing at our gloppy shoe crew.

A lumpy hill becomes our throne,
As worms roll by on a rocky phone.
They call each other, 'Come join the fun!'
'The more, the merrier!'—says the dung beetle run.

## Abode of the Ancients

Old boots of gnomes lie buried deep,
While squirrels hold secrets they'll never keep.
With roots entwined in puzzles untold,
They host a story of soil so bold.

The mighty oak was once a sprout,
Now stands tall while critters shout.
'Long live the tree!' the grasses yelp,
As bugs perform their acrobatic help.

## The Depths of Nurture

A mole with a hat thinks he's quite the chef,
Cooking mud pies, he can't help himself.
While ladybugs place tiny bets,
On who'll win in this soil game's sets.

With roots like spaghetti, oh what a sight,
They tangle and laugh 'til the fall of night.
The earthworms wink with a wink so sly,
'Come join our feast, don't be shy!'

### **Roots Unfurled**

In the garden where veggies thrive,
Carrots giggle, and cabbages jive.
Beets wear pants with stripes so bold,
While radishes tell stories of old.

Worms hold concerts beneath the earth,
With soil as their stage, oh what mirth!
A cabbage keeps rhythm with a beat,
As moles tap dance with tiny feet.

## A Place to Flourish

A flower sneezed, the pollen flew,
And daisies laughed, oh what a view!
Tomatoes play hide and seek all day,
While peas make puns in their green ballet.

Frogs wear hats with stylish flair,
Mice in toques prepare a fair.
And birds critique their fashion scene,
As butterflies dance, all bright and keen.

## Whispers of the Ground

The soil sings secrets, soft and low,
"Plant your dreams, let them grow!"
Ants throw parties with crumbs so sweet,
While beetles play horns, oh what a treat!

Roots gossip about the latest trend,
"Who's the flower that's hard to bend?"
Grass rolls its eyes at the weeds' loud talk,
As earthworms giggle on their little walk.

## Beneath the Canopy of Stars

At night the critters gather 'round,
Under the stars, with poppy sound.
Crickets share tales, quite hilarious,
While fireflies dance, oh so various!

The moon grins down on this lively scene,
"Who knew dirt could be so very keen?"
Laughter erupts in the leafy gloom,
As nature hosts its own wild bloom.

## Cradle of Fertility

In the garden, worms do wiggle,
Spreading joy with every giggle.
Plants all dance in grow-some glee,
While bugs hold a wild jubilee.

Compost piles are the talk of town,
Funky smells won't bring you down.
Roots all chat like neighbors would,
Sharing gossip, oh so good!

Beneath the sun, we all do play,
Digging dirt on a sunny day.
Moles are plotting, oh so sly,
While daisies wave their heads up high.

Nature's playground, full of cheer,
A slip of mud brings no great fear.
With spades in hand, we all agree,
Soil's more fun than it should be!

## Hallowed Ground

In every yard, a secret scheme,
Flowers hatch a blooming dream.
Grass blades gossip, tall and green,
Sharing tales of the unseen.

A caterpillar, oh so bold,
Thinks he's the king of the world.
With every inch, he takes a stab,
At being quick—he's rather drab!

Ladybugs in a fancy dress,
Holding meetings, no less!
"Let's party by the marigold!"
They always need a place to mold.

Earthworms wiggle, a funky crew,
Digging tunnels day and night too.
Each little clump, a treasure found,
Turn in darkness, far from sound!

## Whispering Loam

Whispers drift from dirt so warm,
Fungus tells of a curious charm.
"Did you see that squirrel's great leap?"
While ants march on, their harvest deep.

The soil sings with each fine rain,
Crickets laugh at their own pain.
"To plant or not?" they question loud,
Feeling merry, far from crowd.

Bees are buzzing day and night,
Deciding which bloom is just right.
A dandelion sighs in jest,
"When's the last time I was a guest?"

No worries here just laid-back fun,
With each soft plop, the joy is spun.
In every crack, a story lives,
As soil chuckles, laughter gives!

## Sanctuary Beneath Our Feet

Beneath our toes, a world of play,
Tiny critters at work each day.
"Step lightly, human!" they declare,
"We're busy here, so don't you dare!"

Mushrooms pop like balloons afloat,
With a wink, they smile and gloat.
"Who knew that dirt could be such fun?"
In our earthy realm, we run!

Peeking roots with their magic spells,
Whisper secrets in their dwells.
Each pebble holds a tale untold,
From days of old, in the soil so bold.

With every dig, a new surprise,
Buried treasures raise their eyes.
Laughing leaves from the shady height,
Celebrate life in soil's delight!

## Beneath the Canopy

In a forest where squirrels chatter,
Leaves giggle, and branches scatter.
Mice dance in a twirling spree,
While mushrooms laugh with glee.

The sun peeks through with a smile,
Each shadow plays hide and seek for a while.
Critters gather, making a fuss,
Claiming spots on the old mossy bus.

A rabbit dons a tiny top hat,
Winks at the bees, all jazzed and fat.
With a wink and a hop, he claims the seat,
Inviting all to join the beat.

The ground shakes as roots wiggle and squirm,
Dancing to the earth's funky term.
Underneath, a party's in full swing,
Nature's chatter as the critters sing.

## The Fertile Cradle

In the dirt, where the veggies plot,
A cabbage dreams of a dance-off hot.
Carrots plan a bright conga line,
While tomatoes sip on sun-soaked wine.

Each seedling stuck in a playful race,
Sprouting leaves with a smiling face.
Radishes pull pranks on the peas,
Chasing away the buzzing bees.

The soil buzzes with a ticklish glee,
As worms wiggle in a jubilee.
Roots twist up, in a tangle of fun,
Celebrating with laughter under the sun.

In this cradle of earth, love is the key,
Sharing secrets with each sprouting spree.
Joy blossoms bright, as plants unite,
Creating a garden of pure delight.

## Heartbeats of the Earth

Listen close, the ground has tales,
Of tiny bugs with grand regales.
Ants march in a parade of cheer,
While grasshoppers play the tambourine near.

Something's buzzing, oh what a sound,
A ladybug wears a crown unbound.
Frogs croak beats from a muddy stage,
As fireflies wink with a glow of sage.

Mushrooms gather for a comedy show,
Jokes about rain and how it will flow.
Under the stars, their laughter grows,
With the earth's heart beating soft in throes.

Each creature sways in this rhythm divine,
With nature's heartbeat, they all entwine.
In this wild cavern of joy and mirth,
Life dances freely, praising the earth.

# Celestial Compost

In a pile where things go green,
Old peels and scraps, quite the scene.
Bananas argue who's the best,
As the leftover pizza takes a rest.

Coffee grounds gossip, what a brew!
Sharing tales of mornings, fresh and new.
Worms wiggle through with their own delight,
Mixing up flavors till day turns to night.

A cabbage leaf tells of dreams so bold,
Of crunchy salads and meals untold.
"Don't forget our newest guest," it says,
"The apple core's got some juicy plays!"

In this compost bin, laughter abounds,
As food scraps gather for merry sounds.
Through the layers, a friendship grows,
In a mix of soil, where humor flows.

## The Comfort of Compost

In the heap where scraps decay,
Worms throw parties every day.
Banana peels and leafy greens,
Create a smell that's fit for queens.

Rabbits hop, the cows all moo,
While beetles dance, the ants all skew.
It's a smelly gala, oh what fun,
Life's a riot when you're done with run!

Turn the pile, give it a spin,
Amazed at all the magic within.
Just keep your nose a little away,
From the grand feast of yesterday!

So here's to dirt, life's favorite friend,
With laughter and joy that never ends.
A home for critters, big and small,
In compost heaven, we laugh and sprawl!

## **Harmony in the Humus**

In the gooey depths of rich, dark land,
Tiny critters play in a band.
Slugs on tambourines, bugs that sing,
A concert where the earthworms swing!

Roots tap dance as they spread so wide,
While mushrooms giggle at the side.
Twirling spores, oh what a sight,
It's a funky garden party delight!

Sunshine beams with a golden grin,
As nature's laughter echoes within.
Like soil's own jazz, it keeps the beat,
In this earthy world, life's oh so sweet!

So join the fun beneath your feet,
Where life turns rotten into a treat.
As laughter sprouts from each tiny fir,
In humus harmony, we all concur!

## Crumbs of Creation

What's that beneath the tomatoes' sway?
A crumbly kingdom where fairies play!
Rice and beans take a joyful leap,
Nature's magic in the soil so deep.

Tiny tots of roots poke their heads,
Searching for crumbs on earthy beds.
A crumb of joy, a sprinkle of cheer,
Makes the garden's laughter loud and clear!

From broken chips to leftover bread,
Beetles munch with laughter, they're fed.
Grinning gophers share a bite,
As compost dances through day and night!

So gather 'round the soil so grand,
Join the fun with a hefty hand.
For every crumb that falls to ground,
Is where the secrets of joy are found!

## **Tilling the Soul**

With shovel in hand, I dig with glee,
Turning the earth, wild and free.
Each turn reveals treasures untold,
A rubber boot's worth of laughter, behold!

Digging deep brings laughter out,
From worms and critters, there's never doubt.
Every clump of dirt holds a smile,
Making gardening feel like a joyful trial!

The soil whispers jokes from long ago,
While plants make puns as they sprout and grow.
Life's a comedy in every patch,
With each till, there's a new catch!

So, let's all get our hands in the muck,
With laughter and joy, we're in for luck.
In fields of green, where giggles roll,
We're tilling not just dirt, but the soul!

## **The Hidden Abode**

In the garden, a gopher takes a nap,
While squirrels dance a silly little tap.
Earthworms wiggle with a wiggle so grand,
Making mud pies with a tiny, slimy hand.

A snail races slow in a shell of delight,
While ants throw a party, oh what a sight!
The roots gossip wildly beneath the ground,
Sharing the secrets that they have found.

Caterpillars munch on leaves with great cheer,
While the daisies chat over tea, I hear.
A beetle rolls ball, like it's all a game,
In this hidden abode, nothing's the same.

With laughter and joy, the soil is alive,
Nature's fun circus where all critters thrive.
Beneath the green shelter, they all join the fun,
In this secretive space, under the sun.

## **Roots entwined**

Roots play tag in a tangle so tight,
They laugh and they jiggle, what a funny sight!
The trees whisper secrets to the grass below,
It's a friendly affair in their earthy show.

A dandelion sneezes, poof! Seeds take flight,
While mushrooms break dance in the pale moonlight.
The daisies join in for a jolly good spin,
In this rooty affair, where chaos begins!

The ferns wear their fronds like a fancy hat,
While the sniffing raccoon says, "What's up with that?"
Critters all gather for a soil-lover's rhyme,
In this tangled ruckus, they all have a prime.

As night falls around, they snicker and sigh,
Roots entwined in laughter, oh my, oh my!
Nature's own party, a lively delight,
In the embrace of the ground, all day and night.

## Nature's Nest

In the heart of the garden, a nest is made,
Filled with nuts, grass, and a trusty old blade.
The sparrows chirp witty in morning light,
While bees buzz around like they're ready for flight.

The raccoon pops by with a mask on its face,
Claiming this nest as a curious space.
The ladybugs giggle at this funny mess,
In Nature's nest, nothing's a stress!

The owl in the tree gives a wise old wink,
While rabbits hop round with a jig and a drink.
Under leaves, they gather, a whimsical team,
Sharing stories of dirt, dreams, and wild schemes.

As dusk drapes the earth in a velvet embrace,
The nest is alive with a cozy, warm grace.
In Nature's nest, joy knows no bounds,
In the light of the moon, laughter resounds.

# Nourishing Clay

In a pot of clay, a tiny seed sleeps,
Dreaming of sun and the rain that it keeps.
With laughter and glee, the raindrops descend,
While the worms cheer them on, oh what a blend!

The muck is a feast for a jumpy young frog,
Who does a backflip, then falls in a bog.
"Oh, I'll stick to the shore," he chuckles in cheer,
In the sloshy old clay, no sign of a fear.

Mice throw a ball in the dark, muddy ground,
While crickets sing songs, a jubilant sound.
With sprigs and with things, all creatures will play,
In the joyful embrace of nourishing clay.

So come one, come all, let's dance on the floor,
In the earth's soft embrace where we laugh and explore.
From the soil we rise, with the sun shining bright,
In the clay's warm hug, everything feels right!

## Essence of the Undergrowth

In a garden where worms do wiggle,
A potato tries to solve a riddle.
"Why do we grow beneath the earth?"
Grumbled, "I'm just here for the worth!"

The carrots laugh with leafy glee,
As radishes giggle, "Oh, let it be!"
They squabble of secrets, of roots and shoots,
While beetles dance in their fuzzy suits.

The radish rolls, a daring feat,
"Just don't get stuck, or face defeat!"
A worm yells out, "Don't be absurd!"
"I can win this race, I'm not deterred!"

At the end, they dig up gold,
A treasure trove of stories told.
In the undergrowth, they sit and jive,
The garden's charm is so alive!

## The Soil's Serenade

Beneath the grass, the critters hum,
While moles and voles beat a merry drum.
The daisies sway, they can't resist,
Joining in on their garden twist!

A weary turnip starts to sway,
"I think I'll nap, just for today!"
The cabbages nod, in leafy cheer,
"Oh, don't be lazy, join the fun here!"

A trowel named Tim has a great laugh,
"Why dig alone? Let's do the math!"
With friends in tow, they plant and glean,
Forming the silliest farming scene!

Underneath the sunset glow,
They sing their songs, let laughter flow.
In this patch, where the soil greets,
Life's just a dance on tiny feet!

## Haven of Harvest

In a place where veggies love to spin,
The tomatoes grin, they've got good skin.
Pumpkins puff with juicy delight,
While zucchini dreams take silly flight!

Ah, the onions, oh what a mess,
With layers peeling, they just confess,
"We can't help it, it's in our genes,
To bring the tears on garden scenes!"

The beans do twist with ropes and ties,
Swinging high, in laughter they rise.
"Hey you, squash! Don't be a bore!"
"Join in the fun, don't stay on the floor!"

Harvest time is a rowdy show,
Where roots and fruits dance row by row.
They giggle and wiggle, a veggie parade,
In a haven of harvest, memories made!

## Touched by Tilling

In the till, a big old beet,
Claims he's the star, can't face defeat.
But dirt flings back and says with flair,
"You may be cute, but you're quite bare!"

Tomatoes prance, they call him, "King!"
Yet everyone knows he can't dance or sing.
Potatoes chuckle from underground,
While butterbeans roll, round and round.

Oh what a sight, as they all compete,
To see who can pull the most neat feat.
The radish shows off, so proud and spry,
While the peas thump old beet on the thigh!

When the sun goes down, and shadows fall,
They gather close for the grandest ball.
With dirt on their lips, they laugh in glee,
In this tilled-up world, they're wild and free!

## The Quiet Dirt

In silence, it sits, so very still,
A patch of brown, with an earthy thrill.
Worms hold parties, they groove all night,
While ants play hide and seek out of sight.

They say it listens, oh what a bore,
To plants telling jokes, it begs for more.
With gossipy roots, it shares the good,
Of who's on the rise in the neighborhood!

When raindrops fall, they splash and leap,
Creating mud pies for critters to keep.
Oh, watch out for puddles, they're full of glee,
But your shoes may squeak; oh not again, whee!

And when the sun shines, it laughs with glee,
Tanning like a beachgoer, you see!
So let's raise a glass to this clever ground,
For it's the life of the party, all around!

## Nestled in Nature

In nature's arms, a cozy den,
With roots tickling toes of sleepy men.
The leaves gossip softly, such juicy bits,
About the squirrels and their acorn fits.

Huddled here in a leafy nook,
Raccoons read stories, like a good book.
A rabbit serves tea, in cups of moss,
To the insects, who gossip and never toss!

The sunbeams dance like they've won a prize,
While butterflies waltz under laughter skies.
Be careful, dear friend, don't spill the brew,
For ants gather round; they want some too!

When twilight falls, the weirdness starts,
With fireflies throwing glowstick arts.
A wild serenade from all who reside,
In this quirky corner where joy can't hide!

## Bounty from Below

Down under, the treasures are quite unique,
Gold for the toadstools, or so they speak.
Beetles throw feasts, they've got the knack,
While a caterpillar rolls like it's on track.

The mushrooms giggle, with caps so bright,
Sharing their secrets in dim, soft light.
Carrots with attitudes pop out of doors,
Claiming they're kings of the veggie shores!

The onions weep, they're dramatic, it's true,
While radishes dance like they've drank some brew.
Every root has a tale, a giggle or song,
In this bustling kingdom where veggies belong!

So harvest your laughter, grow joy in your patch,
For down below, there's always a catch.
A bounty of jest, from each tiny plug,
Where fun sprouts up, with the warmth of a hug!

## The Hidden Hearth

In the depths of the garden, a warm little nook,
Where soil meets humor, take a good look.
Worms tell tall tales, they're quite the team,
Singing to seedlings, it's a soil dream!

The roots twist and turn, in a wiggly dance,
While ladybugs giggle, caught in a trance.
They throw tiny balls made of dew and dirt,
Creating a ruckus, in their flower shirts!

A snug little hearth, where earthworms cook,
Their specialty? Grape-flavored muck.
Plants gather 'round for a feast of lies,
While crickets provide their sweet lullabies!

The scent of compost, a fragrant delight,
Beckons the bees for an evening bite.
So let's celebrate this wacky abode,
Where laughter erupts from life's hidden road!

## Grounded Whispers

In the garden, toes all wiggly,
Earthworms giggle, oh so jiggly.
Ladybugs dance with a silly thrill,
While snails take a stroll, oh what a chill!

Plants gossip softly, can you hear?
With beetles chuckling, never a fear.
Flowers wear hats made of dew,
Sipping sun tea, just me and you!

Frogs in boots jump to the beat,
While ants march proudly, oh so neat.
Digging for treasure, a lost shoe found,
Nature's mischief, all around!

In the soil, laughter takes its root,
With every worm, a tiny hoot!
Join the party, don't be slow,
In this mucky, joyful, earthy show!

## The Womb of the Wilderness

In the wild, where critters roam,
Mice wear capes, they feel like home.
Squirrels debate, who steals the nut,
While wise old owls say, "What the fluff?"

The trees wear glasses, reading the breeze,
As raccoons argue, "Who's got the keys?"
Bunny ninjas hop on their quest,
While foxes practice their best jest!

Every root tells tales of woe,
"Why's my acorn not a show?"
But ask a seed, and you'll quickly see,
It's all about the fun and glee!

Underneath the cosmos' dome,
Nature's giggle feels like home.
So grab your shovel, come take a seat,
Let's dance with worms to an earthy beat!

## Mud and Memory

In the puddles, we jump with glee,
Mud pies baking come join me!
Flip-flops squishing, socks a mess,
But in this dirt, we're truly blessed!

Memory lanes paved in clay,
Chasing butterflies, come what may.
Laughter echoes through the muck,
Even when it's all gone amuck!

The ducks quack jokes, it's quite a sight,
As the geese honk with all their might.
With every splash, a story spins,
And laughter in the dirt begins!

So let's embrace this muddy floor,
Who needs sidewalks, when there's more?
In every squish, a world to find,
In muddy memories that are one of a kind!

## Haven of the Heart

In the heart of a garden, stories grow,
With toads croaking songs in a row.
Petunias wink with playful zest,
While bees take turns in a nectar fest!

The sun's warm laugh tickles the trees,
While butterflies flutter, dancing with ease.
A stocky old gopher, wise and neat,
Teaches the young ones to tap dance with feet!

With roots intertwined, friendships bloom,
Every leaf whispers, "There's always room!"
As crickets chirp their evening tunes,
We'll sway through life like gentle balloons!

So in this patch of joy and mirth,
We find our happiness, deep in the earth.
Digging together, let's share our art,
In this delightful haven of the heart!

## Thrumming with Life

In the garden, worms wiggle and squirm,
Telling tales of the soil's warm firm.
Bees buzz around in a slapstick dance,
While ants march on, not missing a chance.

The carrots giggle beneath their hats,
While tomatoes gossip with leaf-clad spats.
A cabbage grins as it takes a seat,
On a lettuce leaf? Oh, what a treat!

Frogs croak puns in the pond's soft glow,
While daisies laugh at the dandelion's show.
Life here is silly, a whimsy parade,
In this place where fondness is made.

So come take a peek, do leave your frowns,
Join the fun in the soil of clowns.
Nature's a jester, a lively buffoon,
In this joyful patch under the moon.

## Echoes of the Underground

Deep below, where the roots take a snooze,
Mole critters chatter, sharing old blues.
Rabbits are rapping, the gophers are beat,
Beneath the surface, they all feel the heat.

Rocks roll their eyes at the ants' silly prance,
While centipedes throw a bug disco dance.
"Hey, this is my turf!" a wise beetle shouts,
As he tries to impress the field-mouse scouts.

Pipes of the soil hum a cheeky tune,
Echoes of life where the critters commune.
A snail slides by, boasting slowest of speeds,
It's the groove of the earth, fulfilling its needs.

So dive down deep, hear the fun and the cheer,
In the underground realm, where laughter is near.
A kingdom of quirks, of frolic and jest,
In the hum of the soil, where nature is best.

## Veins of the Earth

The earth wears a cloak, all wrinkled and wise,
With potatoes plotting beneath leafy skies.
Underneath, where the laughter does flow,
Fungi throw parties, shaking their glow.

"Well, howdy!" says a rock with a crusty old grin,
As a sprout pops up, saying, "Let's begin!"
All the tulips tease the shy roots in the muck,
While the flies spin tales of their everyday luck.

Porcupines poke fun at the worms in their race,
"Can you dig it?"—a rather slow-paced chase.
The moles are the referee, sneaky and sly,
Making sure this muddy match won't go dry.

So dig down deep and let your heart soar,
For the veins of the earth keep the jokes at the core.
In this quirky haven, find joy and delight,
In the playful rhythms of day and of night.

## Enchanted Earth

The soil's alive, oh what a sight,
With mushrooms that giggle and worms that delight.
Sprinklers sashay, dancing with grace,
While raindrops join in, splashing the place.

Ants throw feasts with their crumb-sized cakes,
As the grasshoppers croon with their old-fashioned shakes.
A wise old tree shares its notes of the past,
While flowers sway, caught in laughter's blast.

The sun winks down, playfully bright,
While clouds drift by, a comical sight.
"Why don't we dance?" the wind starts to hum,
As a chorus of nature begins to succumb.

So wander these lands, where the smiles sprout wide,
In this enchanted patch, your heart's open wide.
Giggles and joy mix in earthy delight,
With every step taken, you'll feel pure light.

## Gossamer of the Ground

Beneath the grass, there's quite a show,
A busy world, where the worms do glow.
They wriggle and squirm, what a sight to see,
Stirring up dirt like it's a great jubilee.

Ants hold parades, marching in a line,
While beetles complain of the lack of wine.
The roots of the trees gossip low and sweet,
Sharing secrets of earth that they just can't beat.

A snail in its shell tells tales of the rain,
Of puddles that formed on a stony plain.
With each little droplet, a dance they go,
In the muddy puddle, they put on a show.

Daisies and dandelions have a grand debate,
On which one of them is the true estate.
The soil, it chuckles, for it knows the score,
They all live together, rooting for more!

## Harmony in the Depths

In the depths of the earth, are sounds you won't hear,
As moles sneak around, holding meetings in fear.
The rocks can't eavesdrop, they're too stout and old,
While mushrooms are gossiping, daring and bold.

A squirrel drops nuts, with a plop and a thud,
Where worms have a party, all covered in mud.
The roots serenade with a chorus so sweet,
While spiders send webs through the grass at their feet.

Grasshoppers leap, playing hopscotch with radish,
As carrots play music, it's quite the odd ball dish.
The balanced boogie of life underground,
Keeps tickling the toes of all things around.

Here lies a riot of nature's own art,
Where laughter is planted and friendships start.
The ground is alive with a whimsical cheer,
As microorganisms park for a beer.

## Oasis of Organic Matter

In a patch of rich earth, there's a party tonight,
As compost confetti takes off in delight.
The veggies are waltzing, the bugs join in spree,
In this grand gala, all are welcome to see.

Tomatoes roll by, with a squish and a splash,
While cucumbers giggle and do a fine dash.
The lettuce, it spins, in a pirouette grand,
While carrots applaud with their leafy green band.

The beetroot is blushing, its party dress bright,
As radishes boast they can take on the night.
With every new compost pile, dreams never cease,
Creating a place where legumes find peace.

As twilight descends, and the crickets they sing,
The earthworms digest what the plants give in fling.
In shades of the soil, fun is never drained,
A festival blooms, forever unchained!

## The Resting Place of Seeds

Beneath the soft ground, a slumbering crowd,
Seeds lie in their blankets, snug and proud.
Each one a dreamer with stories to weave,
Waiting for sunshine and rains, they believe.

A sunflower jokes with a shy little pea,
"Will you grow faster or stay slow like me?"
The beans share ambitions of reaching the sky,
While radishes giggle—"We're so close to pie!"

With whispers of roots nudging close for a peek,
The daisies proclaim, "Next week is our week!"
The soil, a sage, just chuckles with glee,
Knowing the secrets it's keeping for free.

As dreams take their place, and darkness takes flight,
The seeds begin stirring, ready for light.
A riot of colors, of life, and of cheer,
In the cozy embrace where their hopes reappear.

## Rhythm of the Riches

In the dirt, a treasure lies,
Wiggly worms wear tiny ties.
They dance around, a funky groove,
Making gardens sway and move.

Plants with hats and roots that wiggle,
Every droplet makes them giggle.
Bees bring news, a buzzing choir,
The flowers bloom, they never tire.

Rabbits hop, they join the show,
Finding snacks in soil below.
With every dig, a surprise found,
A universe spins round and round.

Nature's joke, a playful scheme,
The earthy bed, a funny dream.
So laugh along as growth unfolds,
In rich, brown dirt, just watch the golds.

## The Bounty Below

Digging deep for fun and cheer,
Potatoes wink and shout, 'We're here!'
Carrots hide and tease your eyes,
They giggle, dressed in earth disguise.

Turnips prance in leafy hats,
Cabbages chat with garden rats.
They feast on sun and rain's embrace,
Creating smiles in this wild space.

With every scoop, surprise awaits,
A treasure trove of funny mates.
Beans crack jokes, they sway and sing,
The bounty's dance, a joyful fling.

So come and join the playful plight,
Where roots and sprouts invite delight.
In the depths, a party grows,
The bounty laughs, and everyone knows!

## Cultivating Calm

In the garden, laughter grows,
Gnome hats bobbing, who knows who knows!
Sunshine whispers soft and clear,
While squishy mud brings forth a cheer.

Worms debate, the earth's best crew,
Who can wiggle more than you?
Each tiny seed with dreams to sow,
Crammed with jokes, they steal the show.

Daisies sway, they start to hum,
Telling tales of where they're from.
The daisies giggle, 'We're always neat!'
In rows of laughter, they have a seat.

Peaceful dirt, where silliness thrives,
Harvesting joy, oh how it drives!
Dig into humor, let it bloom,
In every pot and corner room.

## Nest of the Nurtured

In cozy beds where seedlings snore,
Mice throw parties, they want more!
Chickens cluck their plans for tea,
With peas and radishes as company.

Sunshine beams like a silly grin,
Tickling leaves, inviting in.
The roots dance wildly to the beat,
As flowers' giggles can't be beat.

Wiggly sprouts play peek-a-boo,
Punchlines hiding under dew.
The garden's heart, a joyful song,
Where all the funny creatures throng.

So plant your laughter in the ground,
Join the sun-kissed, playful crowd.
In every nook, a smile's made,
Nestled deep where dreams invade.

# Echoes of the Subterranean

In the quiet depths, worms hold a feast,
Chasing their dreams, toast on a yeast.
Tiny roots dance, tip-tap to the beat,
With dirt as their disco, life feels so sweet.

Mud pies are crafted, oh what a delight,
Gourmet meals served under the moonlight.
Gophers gossip, in whispers so sly,
Sharing the news of the slow-rolling pie.

The ants form a line, a parade that seems grand,
Marching in rhythm, each with cake in hand.
Their soil is a banquet, a smorgasbord twist,
Life underground feels like a funny little gist.

Rabbits savor the veggies, oh what a sight,
In this underground realm, nothing's uptight.
Each root a delight, each bug a surprise,
In the echoes below, laughter never dies.

## The Keeper of Nourishment

A quirky old gnome with a hat that's too tall,
Wanders the garden, where whispers enthrall.
"Fertilize with freckles!" he chortles with glee,
His jokes make the daisies burst out in spree.

With gloves made of cabbage and boots of soft clay,
He tickles the soil, come join in the play!
"Don't squash my young seedlings!" he giggles and spins,

As purple-haired turnips start dancing like twins.

He talks to each beet, with a joke or a pun,
"A root a day keeps the sadness all done!"
He dreams of a banquet where plants wear a crown,
Holding a feast in his whimsical town.

The whispers of veggies, the chuckles of mud,
Turn every harvest into a real flood.
In his garden of joy, all spirits set free,
Each shovelful of laughter grows joyfully.

## Cradled in Compost

There's magic in muck, a gooey delight,
Where banana peels dream of flying at night.
Worms gather round, with conference in sight,
Debating the merits of soggy old bite.

A coffee ground castle, with grounds for a moat,
Where every old scrap is a quirky new quote.
Eggshells tell tales of a fine morning brew,
While moldy old bread cracks a smile, "I still do!"

The leaves take a bow, as the worms start to sing,
Praising the art of the composting bling.
"Come, party with us, in this earthy surprise,
Wear your organic best, we'll compost the skies!"

Mirth glows in heaps, in the soft, fertile ground,
As laughter rises high from what's buried around.
In this quirky fortress of decay and delight,
Old scraps become stories that twinkle at night.

## Earth's Tender Embrace

In the arms of the earth, they giggle and play,
Dust bunnies swirl in a whimsical way.
With roots intertwined, they hold hands and sway,
In this cozy blanket, where worries decay.

Dandelion dreams are brewed in the mist,
Hiccups from radishes, all make a twist.
With each plucky sprout, a new friend arrives,
In the garden of chuckles, where silliness thrives.

The rocks join the party, a grumpy old crew,
But laden with puns, they chuckle right through.
They toss dirt like confetti, out playful and spry,
In this earthy embrace, they all reach for the sky.

Beneath sunny smiles, shenanigans brew,
With compost confessions, they giggle anew.
In this merry patch, old and young twirl around,
Earth's tender embrace in laughter is found.

## Life Beneath the Layers

Worms wear suits, they wiggle and dance,
In a hidden world, they'll take a chance.
Beneath the surface, secrets they keep,
While ants form parades—one big, hungry heap.

Mice in tuxedos throw parties at night,
With cheese on the table, they munch with delight.
They gossip of roots and the bugs that they meet,
While the moles are just snoozing, they can't take the heat.

Grubs tell tall tales of their glorious dreams,
Of crawling on gardens and wandering streams.
With laughs that can shake, they are never shy,
Singing the tunes of the worms up high.

So next time you dig, don't think it's all dirt,
There's a wild nightlife—some skirts and a shirt!
From beetles on roller skates to toads at the bar,
The soil's a dance floor, it's wild and bizarre.

## Heartbeats of the Ground.

The thump of the earth, can you hear the beat?
Crickets tap dancing on little green feet.
Rabbits in jazz shoes, they groove with delight,
While the snails in the back play it mellow and light.

Bees buzzing low, in a high-stakes game,
Who can pollinate first? It's the thrill of the fame!
With daisies as judges, the critters are keen,
A talent show champion, that's the point of the scene.

Potatoes in tuxedos, they prance in a row,
While carrots in top hats steal every show.
And up on the surface, we can only assume,
That laughter erupts from each little bloom.

So remember, dear friend, beneath your bare feet,
There's a party of life that's just hard to beat!
With a waltz of the worms and a beat of the bugs,
Beneath every layer, there are heartbeats and hugs.

## Roots of Refuge

The roots throw a party, then tell us they're shy,
But whisper, "Come join us, oh please don't be dry!"
With popcorn and radishes all in a heap,
They chuckle at gophers who can't take a leap.

Trotting on tubers, the turnips declare,
"We're the best dancers, and no one compares!"
With heads held up high, they twirl and they spin,
While potatoes shout out, "Hey, can we win?"

The beets wear their crowns, they're the royal invite,
With carrots as court jesters, bringing sheer delight.
The roots play a game of 'who's buried the best,'
While mushrooms just watch and take a good rest.

So if life feels heavy and times feel too rough,
Remember the roots—things can be silly and tough!
A refuge awaits in the layers so deep,
Where laughter grows wild, and secrets can creep.

## Earth's Embrace

A hug from the ground, it's a squishy delight,
Where critters are playmates each day and each night.
The snails glide with grace, doing spins as they go,
And mushrooms join in, putting on a grand show.

The daisies hold hands, forming chains in the sun,
With giggles and fireworks—oh, what a fun!
While beetles in shades relax by the pond,
Wishing for puddles to frolic beyond.

While grasshoppers sing, in a tune that is sweet,
The soil keeps the secrets, a magical treat.
With roots all a-dancing, in parties all grand,
And laughter erupting from all over the land.

So sink in the softness, let earth be your guide,
In the heart of the ground, you'll find joy deep inside.
With a world full of wonders, and giggles that soar,
The earth's warm embrace will always welcome more.

**Cellar of Seasons**

In the cellar where dirt dreams bloom,
Worms throw disco parties, igniting gloom.
Rats wear sunglasses, sipping on wine,
Roots dance in rhythm, feeling quite fine.

Potatoes in tuxedos, they steal the show,
Carrots in capes, say, "Look at us grow!"
Tomatoes, blushing, pose for a snap,
While beets are the life of this underground flap.

The turnips chime in with a tap-tap-tap,
As my garden gnomes take a snoozing nap.
Who knew vegetables could hold such a spree,
In this wacky cellar, life's a jubilee?

Every spring brings laughter and a soil shake,
As earthworms throw confetti, watch out for the cake!
It's a cellar of laughter, of jest and of cheer,
Where nature's the comedian, drawing us near.

## Altar of Abundance

Underneath the corn's tall leafy spire,
The squirrels hold meetings by a bonfire.
They plot to steal snacks from human delight,
While beans on the altar bask in moonlight.

The zucchinis gossip, "Who's growing the best?"
As radishes rustle, quite eager for jest.
Broccoli writes poems, not tasty at all,
While cucumbers sip tea, feeling quite small.

The pumpkins wear hats, think it's a fine look,
As beets plot a caper from their cozy nook.
"Let's start a band!" they propose with a cheer,
Their music composed of squelches and sneers.

Yet in this wild altar, there's naught to be fretted,
Just veggies in revels, sweetly embedded.
With carrots as conductors and peas in a row,
Life sprouts up laughter, just watch how it grows!

## The Quiet Pulse of the Planet

In the silent hum of the soil's embrace,
The earthworms gather, clever and ace.
With tiny tophats, they pose for the crowd,
As sprouts take the stage, uncommonly loud.

The daisies declare it a day of great fun,
While fungi juggle, outshining the sun.
A daisy gives birth to a whimsical leaf,
As the roots swap tall tales, devoid of belief.

Beneath all the ruckus, the planet does giggle,
As mulchy mud monsters do twist and do wiggle.
Ants march in chorus, their antlers on show,
Dancing through dirt in a goofy tableau.

Yet silence prevails, like a soft sleepy cat,
As nature delights in this playful habitat.
In the quiet pulse, there's a hint of a grin,
For the earth knows the secrets of laughter within.

## Soil Stories

Gather 'round, dear friends, for tales of the ground,
Where the secrets of soil are giggly and profound.
The turnips tell stories of giants and dreams,
While radishes whisper of daring moonbeams.

"Did you hear the one about the brave old sprout?"
It blended in seamlessly, no doubt about.
The carrots remark, "That's a classic for sure!
We garden dwellers all laugh to the core!"

As acorns tap dance with whimsical grace,
The worms pull the strings in their underground space.
"Let's write a novel," the lettuce proposals,
As weeds weave in to offer some snuggles.

Their stories unfold with laughter and cheer,
In the kingdom of soil, there's naught to fear.
With each little giggle, a tale comes alive,
So, don't underestimate what soil can contrive!

## Cradled by the Clay

In muddy shoes, we dance around,
With earth on our hands, joy abound.
The puddles splash, oh what a sight,
We giggle and laugh, it's pure delight.

Worms play tag beneath our feet,
They wiggle and squirm, so extra sweet.
Digging deep for treasures rare,
We find a toy or just some hair.

In a world of brown, we're kings and queens,
Where dirt is gold, or so it seems.
We make mud pies with a knowing grin,
And crown ourselves with plantains thin.

## Secrets in the Subsoil

What lurks below? We just can't see,
A gopher's party? Oh, let it be!
The carrots giggle, tucked away tight,
"Don't dig us up, it's not polite!"

Worms in tuxedos, oh what a show,
They juggle pebbles, all in a row.
The beetles roll dice, oh how they play,
In a secret world, beneath the clay.

Roots toss a salad, it's quite the feast,
Earthworms cater, not one bit least.
With leafy hats, they cheer and shout,
"Join us in fun, there's no doubt!"

## Hearth of the Humus

Gather 'round the earthy fire,
With jokes aplenty, never tire.
"Who's got the best compost joke?"
"I do!" says Pete, the funny bloke.

From mushroom caps, we serve our drinks,
Stirred with twigs, or so it thinks.
A berry pie made from nature's best,
And crickets chirping, a lively jest.

"Why did the plant blush?" someone sings,
"Because it saw the dirt with wings!"
With laughter loud, we toast and cheer,
In our humble home, no need for fear.

## Beneath the Boughs

Under leafy roofs, we pitch our tent,
With squirrels around, we feel content.
The roots are tickling as we play,
Oh what a fun, fabulous day!

Butterflies gossip, "Did you hear?
The groundhog's throwing a picnic here!"
We dance with mushrooms and swing with glee,
Beneath the boughs, we feel so free.

A party of ants, they bring the snacks,
Cheddar crumbs and crunchy packs.
With laughter ringing, the day slips by,
In our leafy world, we soar and fly.

## The Essence Within

In the garden, worms dance with glee,
Throwing dirt at the ants, oh me!
Sunflowers gossip, their heads held high,
Chasing the bees as they buzz by.

Raccoons plot mischief under the moon,
While potatoes dream of a vegetable tune.
Carrots stretch, trying to touch the sky,
Hoping their tops won't be the reason to die!

Rabbits on stilts wear hats made of leaves,
Tricking the foxes, oh how it deceives!
But deep underground, the party is real,
With mushrooms that dance, it's quite the big deal!

So, raise a toast with your jack-o'-lantern,
To the soil that giggles and won't stop canterin'.
Celebrate all, bring on the jest,
In our earthy kingdom, we know who is best!

## Dwelling of the Earth

Below the surface, a gopher named Lou,
Throws wild parties; oh, what a view!
With rock music played by the beetles' band,
And moles doing magic with a sleight of hand.

The earthworms are chefs, making muck pies,
While the snails are the judges with glittery eyes.
Sowed in laughter, they spin tales anew,
Of the day that a squirrel wore a tutu!

Roots intertwine, sharing secrets they know,
About how the flowers' gossip tends to grow.
One sunflower painted with polka dot flair,
Claims it's the trendiest, but we all know it's rare!

So come join the fun with the critters below,
Where dirt is the currency and laughter the flow.
With each little worm moving in sync,
This is where magic becomes the real link!

# Sphere of Nourishment

In a bowl of soil, dreams start to brew,
Radishes wearing tiny, red shoes.
They gossip with beans, who think they're quite chic,
"Have you heard our fashion's the latest technique?"

Potatoes hold court, they're royalty here,
Dressed in their skins, drawing everyone near.
Grasshoppers serve tea from leaves that they choose,
While a king-sized radish plays blues on his snooze.

Here, the daisies wear crowns made of grit,
While the bumblebees hum, "We're fancy and fit!"
Butterflies twirl in their festival gowns,
Spreading smiles and giggles across leafy towns.

With every rainfall, the laughter grows loud,
As roots tell the tales of the garden's proud crowd.
So next time you dig, remember to grin,
In this earthling soirée, you're always welcome in!

## Breath of the Underground

Dirt devils swirl in a muddy ballet,
While garden gnomes giggle at critters at play.
A snail has a mustache, oh what a sight!
Sipping for hours, he stays up all night.

In the land of the buried, secrets unfold,
Potato spies plotting with roots full of gold.
They plot with the weeds, it's a spectacular scene,
Whispers of mischief, like laughs from a queen.

Tiny mushrooms wear capes, flexing their might,
Challenging beetles to a no-hold fight.
Worms in tuxedos rolling out the red,
Charm all the daisies, who hang by their thread.

So dive in the dirt, find humor and snacks,
Join the raucous theatre behind all the cracks.
Where laughter and roots form a bond that won't break,
The best jokes are planted; it's all for fun's sake!

## Crumbs of Creation

In gardens where gnomes do roam,
The veggies grumble, far from home.
Each carrot tells a joke of cheer,
While worms throw parties, oh so near.

Seeds gossip low beneath the ground,
They chuckle softly, all around.
A radish boasts of size and flair,
While turnips tease, "We dare not share!"

The squash is skewered, finds it funny,
The sun's wink warms them, sweet as honey.
Potatoes giggle, snug in their beds,
Life's full of laughter, no room for dreads.

In this patch of dirt and roots entwined,
Nature plays pranks, so sweet and kind.
With each new sprout, a joke will bloom,
In crumbs of creation, there's plenty of room!

## The Breath of the Buried

Deep within, the secrets lie,
With whispers floating, oh so spry.
Each buried potato gives a shout,
"We bring the nutrients, what's this about?"

Laughter echoes through the loam,
As earthworms wiggle, far from home.
They dream of lettuce, crisp and bright,
With visions of salad, a true delight.

Fungi dance with mycelium grace,
Sharing the dirt, they set the pace.
Rocks chuckle softly, they know the score,
For roots will tickle your toes and more!

In this realm, nothing's stark,
The buried breath brings humor to the dark.
From the depths of the ground, a whimsy unearths,
Where even compost can giggle in mirth!

## **Fertile Whispers**

In the compost, secrets brew,
Banana peels chat with beans so blue.
Cabbage chuckles at the snooty kale,
While sprouts sing out a joyous tale.

Earthworms wiggle and twist with glee,
Piping up, "We're the best you see!"
Life below is a jest-filled fest,
Where every compost heap's truly blessed.

A shy little sprout peeks from the dirt,
Saying, "Watch out, I'm no mere flirt!"
Radishes giggle, "What's in a name?"
"Just roots that play this silly game!"

In laughter's embrace, all plants unite,
Whispering joy through day and night.
In fertile whispers, they find their song,
Where humor grows, and none is wrong!

## Harmony in the Hummus

In bowls of hummus, smooth and grand,
Chickpeas chuckle—"A lovely band!"
Olive oil winks, a tasty friend,
As garlic whispers, "Let's not pretend!"

With each dip, a giggle spreads,
As pita pockets tell of bread.
"You're flat-out funny!" the veggies tease,
"We've got the crunch; just give us ease!"

Salsa swirls in a dance divine,
While carrots boast, "We're feeling fine!"
A sprinkle of humor, a dash of spice,
In this bowl of joy, everything's nice.

So gather round this tasty cheer,
Hummus hugs bring smiles near.
In harmony, flavors join the fun,
Together they shine, like the midday sun!

www.ingramcontent.com/pod-product-compliance
Lightning Source LLC
Chambersburg PA
CBHW070323120526
44590CB00017B/2803